Instant Idea Book

Motivating Your Students

- Creating a Positive Learning Environment
  (pages 6-20)

- Sharing Responsibility
  (pages 21-35)

- Building Self-Esteem
  (pages 36-62)

(includes reproducible pages)

by

Barbara Gruber & Sue Gruber

Illustrations by

Lynn Conklin Power

©Frank Schaffer Publications, Inc.   FS-8310 Motivating Your Students

Copyright© 1987 Frank Schaffer Publications, Inc.
All rights reserved - Printed in the U.S.A.
Published by **Frank Schaffer Publications, Inc.**
1028 Via Mirabel, Palos Verdes Estates, California 90274

ISBN #0-86734-072-X

Table of Contents

Introduction

Motivating Your Students provides strategies to help your students become motivated, independent learners. Our easy-to-implement activities develop confidence and self-control, while fostering self-esteem.

This book will help you build a sense of community and create a classroom where learning is an exciting, positive experience for everyone.

Barbara Gruber

Create a Positive Learning Environment

It's easy to provide a setting for success in your classroom. Small changes in routines or classroom layouts can increase students' motivation, interest and enthusiasm.

Classroom Layouts

Experiment with different furniture arrangements until you find the ones that work best for you! Ask students for opinions and suggestions.

To save time, plan your new classroom layout on paper! Write each student's name on a self-stick note. Move the names around on a seating chart until you have students arranged in a workable pattern. This seating chart will come in handy for substitutes and can be reused when you want to assign students to different seats.

A variety of classroom layouts are provided on pages 8 through 12. Adapt the layouts to fit your classroom dimensions and teaching style.

FS-8310 Motivating Your Students

Classroom Layouts

A Traditional Arrangement

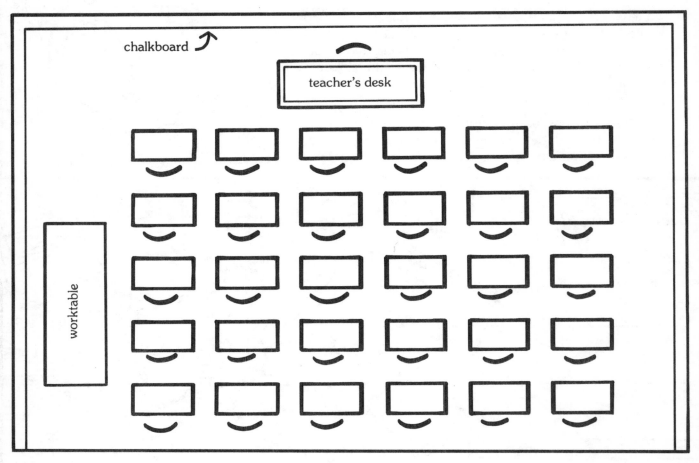

chalkboard

teacher's desk

worktable

Advantages
- It's well suited to whole class instruction.
- All students face you and the chalkboard.
- It's easy for you to monitor students.
- It discourages copying and talking between students.

Disadvantages
- It lacks open areas for group activities.
- It tends to isolate students.

Variations
- Locate your desk at the side or the rear of the room.
- Push desks together in pairs for partner activities.
- Move worktable to the front or the rear of the room.

Classroom Layouts

A Team Arrangement

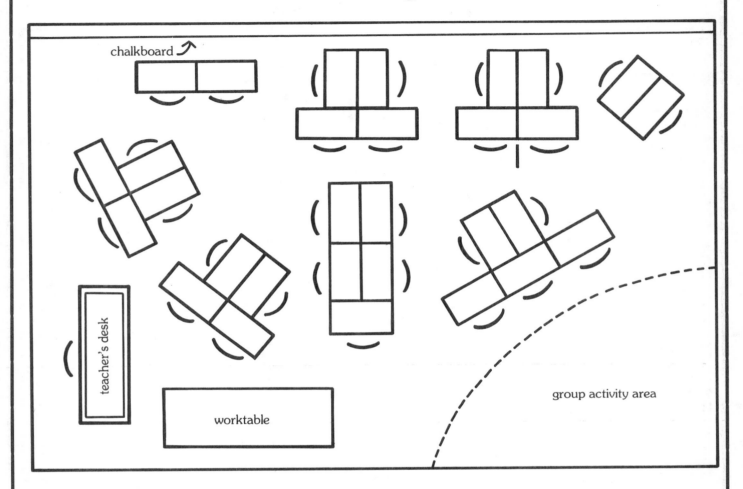

Advantages

- It creates open space for movement and group activities.
- The activity area can be used by students working on tasks that may distract others.
- All students can see the chalkboard.
- It encourages cooperative learning with partners.
- A group of team leaders can distribute and collect materials.
- It's conducive to group work.

Disadvantage

- It's easier for students to copy and talk to others.

Variations

- Locate your desk at the front, rear or center of the room.
- Move the group activity area to the center or front of the room.
- Locate the worktable at the center, front or side of the room.

A Double Semi-Circle Arrangement

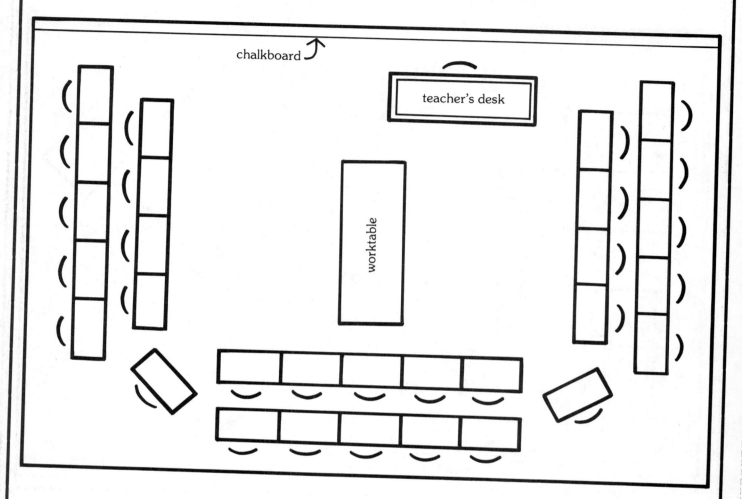

chalkboard

teacher's desk

worktable

Advantages

- It's well suited to class or group instruction.
- All students can see you and the chalkboard.
- It provides an open area for group activities.
- It facilitates communication for class discussions and meetings.
- The worktable can be moved to create a central open area.

Disadvantage

- It's easy for students to copy and talk to others.

Variations

- Move your desk to the side, rear or center of the room.
- Move the worktable to the front, rear or side of the room.

Classroom Layouts

A Space-Maker Arrangement

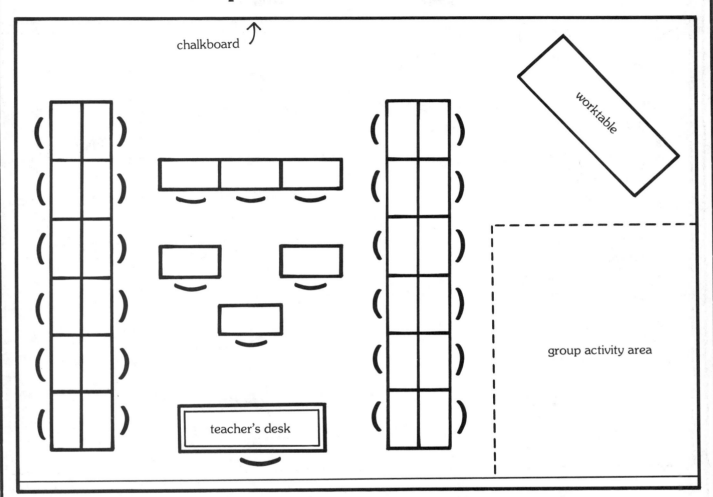

chalkboard

worktable

group activity area

teacher's desk

Advantages
- It's well suited to class or group instruction.
- All students can see the chalkboard.
- Students who need to work alone can be seated in the center.
- It provides a large open area for group activities.
- The activity area can be used by students working on tasks that may distract others.

Disadvantage
- It's easy for students to copy and talk to others.

Variations:
- Locate your desk at the side or front of the room.
- Locate the group activity area at the front or rear of the room.
- Locate the worktable at the front of the room.

A Student-Generated Arrangement

Tell students you are going to let them arrange their desks. Stress that they must choose a location for their desks where they can work without disruption. Give students time to think about and discuss with classmates where they would like to sit. You will discover that some students want to be part of a group while others choose to sit alone.

When the student-generated arrangement is in place, try it for several weeks before making adjustments. The student-generated arrangement works best toward the middle of the school year when students know each other better. Students feel important because the teacher trusts them to make a wise decision about where they sit.

Add a Special Touch!

Make your classroom an attractive place to learn! Ask friends, neighbors and students' parents for items they may wish to donate to the class.
Add a special touch with:

- plants
- posters
- mobiles
- artwork
- area rug
- pillows
- carpet squares
- bean bag chairs
- rocking chair
- reclining chair

Establishing Classroom Routines

Standard procedures for routine classroom tasks, such as tallying lunch counts, taking attendance, and collecting homework are valuable for yourself and your students!

Established procedures will:
- free you from time-consuming, daily clerical tasks
- give students the responsibility for carrying out routine classroom tasks
- motivate students because you have put them in charge of important classroom routines
- save valuable time because you do not have to direct students and answer questions about procedures
- organize the classroom so that you and your students can function more efficiently
- result in fewer lost papers and mix-ups
- create a spirit of cooperation in the classroom

Consider establishing procedures for:
- entering and leaving the classroom
- collecting homework and notes
- sharpening pencils
- getting drinks of water
- using the restrooms
- getting help from you
- taking attendance and lunch counts
- passing out and collecting work and materials

Establishing Classroom Routines

Taking Attendance and Lunch Counts

Make a check-in chart using tagboard and clothespins. Use a felt pen to print students' names on the clothespins. Arrange the clothespins in alphabetical order by students' names and then number them. (This makes it easy for each student to locate his pin.)

At the beginning of every school day, each student moves his clothespin from the "I'm absent" section to the "I'm here today!" or "I'm buying lunch!" sections. After all students have checked in, you can quickly record absences and tally the lunch count by looking at the check-in chart.

Later in the day, have a student helper return the clothespins to the "I'm absent!" section so the check-in chart is ready-to-use the next day.

Collecting Finished Work

- Provide one work box for all finished work.
- Provide a box for each group or subject so work is sorted.
- If students are seated in groups or rows, a group leader can be responsible for collecting finished work from the group.
- Assign each student a number which corresponds to her placement in the grade book. When she hands in her paper, she writes her assigned number in the upper right hand corner and places her paper sequentially—all the papers will be in the correct order to record as they are graded. Any missing work can be easily spotted.

FINISHED WORK

FS-8310 Motivating Your Students

Establishing Classroom Routines

Teaching Classroom Routines

Don't overwhelm your students by introducing too many new routines at once. It is best to teach only one new routine every few days.

- Explain the importance of the procedure being taught.

- Take time to thoroughly teach each procedure.

- Provide ample time to practice the new routine until it goes smoothly.

- Reteach a procedure if it is not being carried out to your standards.

Hill School Library Rules
1. Quiet! Others are reading.
2. You may check out 6 books.
3. Do not remove cards from their pockets.
4. Use bookmarks.
5. Keep our books clean.

Reinforcing Classroom Routines and Rules

Take photographs of your students performing daily class routines. Make certain each student appears in at least one photograph. Post photographs on a bulletin board with a caption as shown.

We clean our paintbrushes.

We raise our hands!

We wait our turn.

A Variety of Learning Situations

Students will benefit from working alone, with partners, and as group members. Therefore, it is important to provide a daily balance of classroom learning situations. Change the pace by following a group activity with an independent work project.

Working Independently

Advantages

- It fosters self-reliance.
- It builds self-confidence.
- Students can work at their own pace.
- Tasks can be tailored to each student.

Disadvantages

- Students may feel isolated.
- Cooperation and communication skills are not used.

Working With Others

It's easy for students to help one another when they work in pairs. Try the partner approach for an art project, spelling practice, math flash cards, or oral reading.

Advantages

- Cooperative learning takes place.
- Students work toward group goals.
- Students learn to take leadership roles.
- Listening skills are developed.
- Students must communicate their ideas to the group.
- Students are exposed to each other's ideas.

Disadvantages

- You must make sure groups are on task.
- Some students may not participate fully.

FS-8310 Motivating Your Students

A Variety of Learning Situations

New Faces and Special Places

It's exciting and motivating to have a guest teacher or to conduct a lesson in a different setting. Try these ideas!

- Invite another teacher or the principal to teach a lesson in your room.
- Invite a guest speaker from the community to address specific student needs, such as a police officer to talk about bicycle safety.
- Have a parent share his or her expertise with the class.
- Take your students to the school library for a special project.
- Read a story to your class outdoors on a nice day.
- Trade places with another teacher and teach a lesson to each other's class.

Communication Counts!

Open lines of communication between parents, students, and teachers create a positive learning climate!

Classroom Journal

Use a notebook for a classroom journal. At the end of each school day, have a student write a few sentences about the events of the day. Give the responsibility for writing in the journal to a different student each day. For primary grades, the teacher can elicit a few sentences from the class to write in the journal. Display the journal at Open House for parents to enjoy!

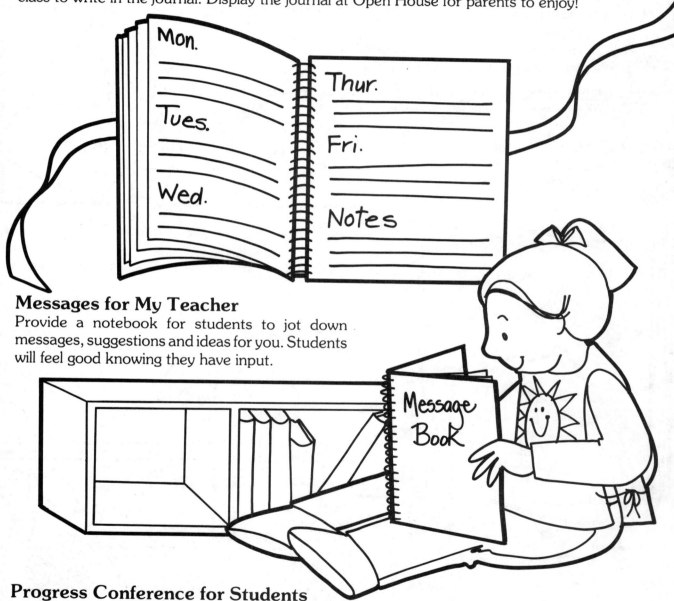

Messages for My Teacher

Provide a notebook for students to jot down messages, suggestions and ideas for you. Students will feel good knowing they have input.

Progress Conference for Students

Just before sending home report cards, schedule a brief conference with each student. Show the student her report card and briefly discuss how you determined her grades. Make sure to have your grade book there in case a student wishes to see her record. This progress conference helps students understand the technical aspects of grading and informs them of their achievements and of areas needing improvement.

Communication Counts!

Say What You Feel!

The best way to communicate is in an open and honest manner. Express your feelings using this non-reproachful technique. It allows you to clearly state how you feel without putting the listener on the defensive. This method works equally well in positive and negative situations.

The pattern is "I feel...when..."

For example:

"I feel happy when you work quietly."

"I feel disappointed when you do not follow directions."

Everyone Participates!

When conducting an oral lesson with your class, do you notice that the same few students always respond? Try this technique to increase participation.

Ask the group a question. When a few students raise their hands, tell the class that you are waiting for a specific student to raise his or her hand. Do not reveal that student's name until almost every student has his hand raised and is ready to answer the question.

Building Class Spirit

Stimulate class spirit to achieve increased cooperation and enthusiasm!

Our Class Mascot

A large stuffed animal makes a perfect mascot for your class.
Add to the fun by:

- having students choose a name for the mascot

- creating a special place for the mascot in the classroom (a chair, desk, cardboard house...)

- dressing the mascot (a Halloween mask, a green hat for St. Patrick's Day, badges, buttons...)

- including the mascot in class parties, open house, and other special happenings

Use the mascot as a reward for individual students or the entire class. Students can hold the mascot during story time, have the mascot on their desk, or make something for the mascot.

Sharing Responsibilities

You can create a climate that fosters independence and self-control in your classroom. Students need to feel that they have an active role in the learning process. They must share with you the responsibility for making progress at school. A sense of responsibility is fostered when students are self-reliant and have opportunities to make decisions.

Fostering Self-Reliance

Create a climate in your classroom that encourages individual responsibility.

Time to Go!

Most teachers are too busy to constantly remind students to go to speech therapy, remedial reading or dental appointments. Give students the responsibility for keeping track of out-of-class schedules and appointments.

For primary students, attach a clock face to the student's desk. In intermediate grades, write the schedule on an index card and attach it to the student's desk.

Schedule

9:20-10:00 Silent Reading

11:00-11:15 Speech

1:10-2:00 Math

SPEECH CLASS

MONDAY-TUESDAY

Here it is!

No Name Folder

The "No Name" Folder

Label a file folder "No Name." After grading papers, place papers without names in the file folder. Explain to students that all papers without names will be placed in the "No Name" folder. Establish a permanant place for the file that is accessible to students. Students are responsible for checking the file for missing papers. At the end of each week, month, or quarter discard the contents of the folder.

Fostering Self-Reliance

Work-to-Do Reminder Notes

Help students keep track of unfinished work and homework assignments with a reminder note! Reproducible "Work-to-Do" reminders are on page 24. These notes help organize students who tend to forget assignments or have difficulty keeping track of assigned work.

Reminder notes keep parents informed of work that must be completed. They also come in handy for students who have missed work due to appointments or illness.

At the end of each school day, students who have a Work-to-Do note list the lessons they must finish. Then you initial the note. At home, parents sign the note after the child has completed the work. The note and the finished work are returned to school the next day.

Why not duplicate the Work-to-Do reminders on a special color paper? This makes them easy to spot and harder to misplace!

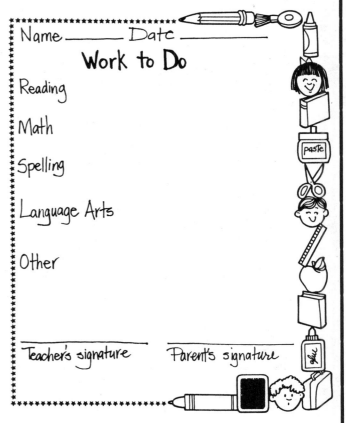

Name _____ Date _____

Work to Do

Reading

Math

Spelling

Language Arts

Other

Teacher's signature   Parent's signature

Take Me Home Today!

Do your students forget to take home notices, books and homework? Solve this problem by establishing a place for each student to put items that must go home. Choose a location near the exit.

At the end of every period, students place books or papers that must go home in their "mailboxes." Before they go home, students remove material from the mailboxes and line up. Glance at the mailboxes to see that all students have their materials.

Name _____ Date _____

Work to Do

Reading

_____

_____

Math

_____

_____

Spelling

_____

_____

Language Arts

_____

_____

Other

_____

_____

_____

_____   _____
Teacher's signature   Parent's signature

a reproducible page   FS-8310 Motivating Your Students

Fostering Self-Reliance

Students need to know that you trust them to make decisions. Provide opportunities for your students to make appropriate choices.

What's Best for You?

Increase students' motivation by occasionally giving them a choice as to how they practice a particular skill. Students can choose the activity that best suits the way they learn.
For example:

I Need Extra Practice!

Ask students to let you know if they need extra practice. Tell students they can request an extra practice worksheet in areas of difficulty. For example, if a student has difficulty with word problems during the math period and requests extra practice, give her a supplemental worksheet on word problems.

If you have a few extra copies of a reproducible worksheet, tell students the copies are available for extra practice.

Fostering Self-Reliance

"I Want to Learn..."

Make a writing booklet with a construction paper cover for each student. At the beginning of each month, have every student set an "I want to learn..." goal for the month and write it in the booklet. Then students can list ways to meet their goal. At the end of the month, have students evaluate their progress.

Who Is Responsible?

Have a class discussion about making choices and fulfilling responsibilities. On a worksheet, list activities performed daily by most children. Ask students to indicate on the worksheet the person responsible for each activity. After responses are on the worksheets, elicit answers from students for group discussion.

Who Is Responsible?				
Task	I am	My mom is	My dad is	My brother or sister is
wake up				
make bed				
pack lunch				
ready on time				
bring things to school				
doing homework				
feeding pets				
going to bed on time				

Looking Back

During the last week of school, have students think about the many skills they have learned during the school year. Students select the skill they think most important. They each write a few sentences describing the skill and telling why it is important. Every child adds an illustration to her description!

Provide an opportunity for students to share their ideas and drawings with the class or with a partner!

Delegating Responsibility

Give your students opportunities for leadership in your classroom. Try this approach!

Class Officers

Every week choose a new class officer for your classroom. All students will benefit from a leadership experience.

Write the name of each office and its duties on a large index card as shown. The first day of each week select a different student to fill each office and write that student's name on the back of the card.

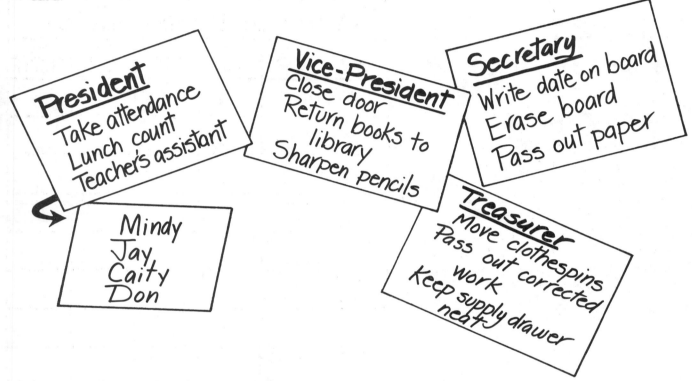

At the beginning of each week, have the previous week's class officers come to the front of the classroom. Each officer chooses someone to take his office. The student looks at the names on the back of the card to make sure he chooses someone who has not yet held that office. You may want to make a rule that boys must pick girls to follow them in office and girls must pick boys.

Being a class officer is voluntary. After all students who wish to serve have had a turn, they may be chosen again.

Delegating Responsibility

Make things go smoothly in your classroom by using your students as assistants!

Tutors

Let students who have mastered a skill help others. Write the tutors' names and their areas of expertise on the board. Other students can go to the right person for assistance!

Try It My Way!

Encourage students to share clever short cuts and tips they have discovered that make learning easier! Ask the student to describe the idea to you. If you feel it would be beneficial to others, have the student teach the class. For example, one student might share with the class finger-math techniques for multiplication facts.

Teacher's Helper

Employ teacher's helpers whenever possible. After giving a spelling test, have a student quickly reread the list of words aloud to the group before collecting papers. Or, ask a student to keep track on a class list of those students who have presented news reports or sharing.

Involving Your Students

It's Up to You!

Increase interest by giving students an opportunity to make choices.

- If you are teaching letter writing, let students choose to whom they write their letters.
- During an art lesson, have two projects available. Students choose the one they wish to make.
- On handwriting assignments, let students select their best papers for you to grade.
- Give students a choice of two similar drill worksheets to do.

Caring About Our Classroom

Encourage students to help make the classroom an attractive place to learn. Students can make signs, posters and banners to decorate the room. Signs can be made that remind students of class rules and values. The district office, school cafeteria, library, or school office may welcome a sign or banner from your students.

High-Interest Approaches to Learning

Giving students an opportunity to record their progress and make choices builds confidence and adds excitement to any subject.

Charting Our Progress!

This approach can be used at all grade levels with any topic! It's easy to prepare and fun for students to use. Post a butcher paper chart with students' names as shown. Write a list of assignments and activities on the chalkboard for students. As each student completes an activity make a check mark by her name on the chart!

To add interest, you may want to cut symbols from construction paper and paste on the chart to indicate completion of a task. Make symbols that are related to the topics.

Some students will finish sooner than others. Therefore, you may want to include some bonus activities for them.

High-Interest Approaches to Learning

Here are more "Charting Our Progress" ideas. Use "Count Your Points" topics on page 32 for this approach, too!

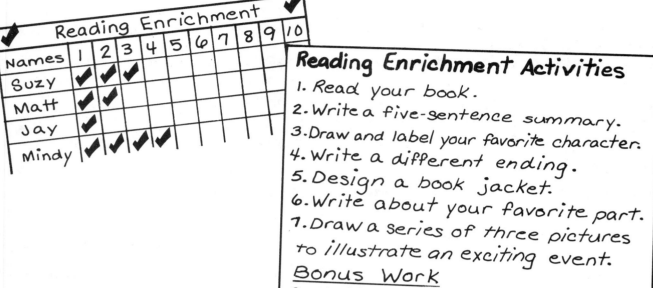

Reading Enrichment

Names	1	2	3	4	5	6	7	8	9	10
Suzy	✔	✔	✔							
Matt	✔	✔								
Jay	✔									
Mindy	✔	✔	✔	✔						

Reading Enrichment Activities
1. Read your book.
2. Write a five-sentence summary.
3. Draw and label your favorite character.
4. Write a different ending.
5. Design a book jacket.
6. Write about your favorite part.
7. Draw a series of three pictures to illustrate an exciting event.

Bonus Work
8. Make a bookmark.
9. Make a mobile.
10. Write a letter to the author.

Famous Americans

Names	1	2	3	4	5	6
Brian	⚑	⚑				
Kevin	⚑	⚑				
Ashley	⚑					
Bonni						

Famous Americans Activities
1. Do famous Americans worksheets.
2. Design a postage stamp.
3. Make a time line.
4. Write a letter to a famous American.

Bonus Activities
5. Find a news article about someone famous.
6. Do an oral report.

High-Interest Approaches to Learning

Count Your Points!

Use this highly motivating approach with any topic! Tell students their grades are based strictly on the number of points they earn. You will provide many different options for earning points so everyone has the opportunity to earn a high grade.

For planning purposes, jot a list of assignments and activities on scratch paper. Keep in mind that the activities and assignments can be teacher directed, completed independently, or a mixture of both. This is an excellent way to integrate the curriculum by including a variety of subjects (reading, art, language...) and activities. If your topic is "Learning About Animals," your list might look like this:

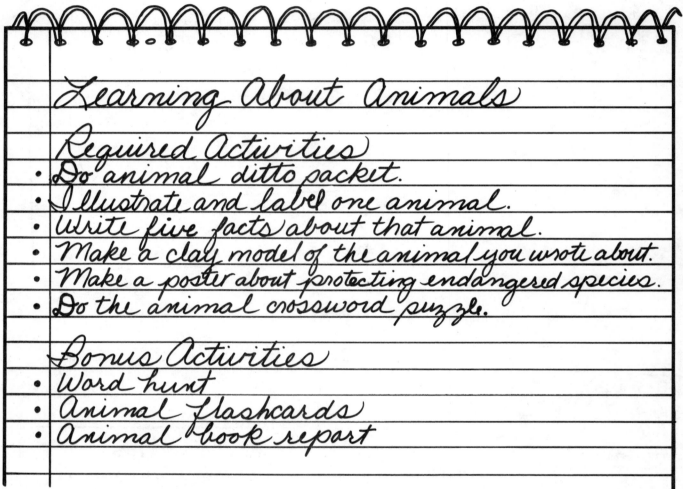

Learning About Animals

Required Activities
- Do animal ditto packet.
- Illustrate and label one animal.
- Write five facts about that animal.
- Make a clay model of the animal you wrote about.
- Make a poster about protecting endangered species.
- Do the animal crossword puzzle.

Bonus Activities
- Word hunt
- Animal flashcards
- Animal book report

After making a list of the activities, assign a point value to each activity. Duplicate the "Count Your Points" assignment sheet using the reproducible format on page 34. Give each student a work folder with the assignment sheet pasted on the front. As students complete an activity, they check it off. Evaluate the work and record the points earned on the student's assignment sheet. Explain to students that the "Points Possible" column shows the maximum that can be earned for perfect work. You will decide how many points the student deserves.

You can use the ideas for "Charting Our Progress" on pages 30 and 31 for the "Count Your Points" approach.

High-Interest Approaches to Learning

Name _Deanna V._   Date Started _2/2_
Topic _Health_   Date Due _2/17_

✓	Required Activities	Points Possible	Points Earned
	Health Book Chapter 5	10	
	Chapter 5 Questions p.45	10	
	Good Nutrition Poster	15	
	Plan a menu for one day	20	
	Food Group Chart	10	
	Sort Food Packages	10	
	Nutrition Quiz	20	
	Bonus Activities		
	Health Filmstrip	10	
	1-Day Food Diary	15	
	Copy healthy Snack Recipe	15	

Total Points Possible _135_

My goal is _____

I earned _____ points.

135-122=A ; 121-108=B ; 107-95=C

Name _Matt F._   Date Started _2/4_
Topic _Learning About Animals_ Date Due _2/13_

✓	Required Activities	Points Possible	Points Earned
✓	Animal Worksheets	15	13
✓	Draw and label an animal. Write 5 facts about it.	10	9
✓	Make a clay model of the animal you wrote about.	15	15
✓	Make a poster about protecting endangered species.	15	14
✓	Do the animal puzzle	15	10
	Bonus Activities		
✓	Do the word hunt	10	10
✓	Write an animal book report	10	9
	Take animal flashcard quiz	10	

Total Points Possible _100_

My goal is _75_

I earned _80_ points.

100-90=A ; 89-80=B ; 79-70=C ; 69-60=D

Name _____ Date Started _____

Topic _____ Date Due _____

✓	Required Activities	Points Possible	Points Earned

Total Points Possible _____

My goal is _____.

I earned _____ points.

FS-8310 Motivating Your Students

High-Interest Approaches to Learning

Desk-Top Checklist

Tape a daily or weekly checklist to each student's desk top. As students complete assignments or activities, they check them off on the Desk-Top Checklist. At the end of the day or week, the checklist can go home as a communication to parents.

Ideas for checklists:

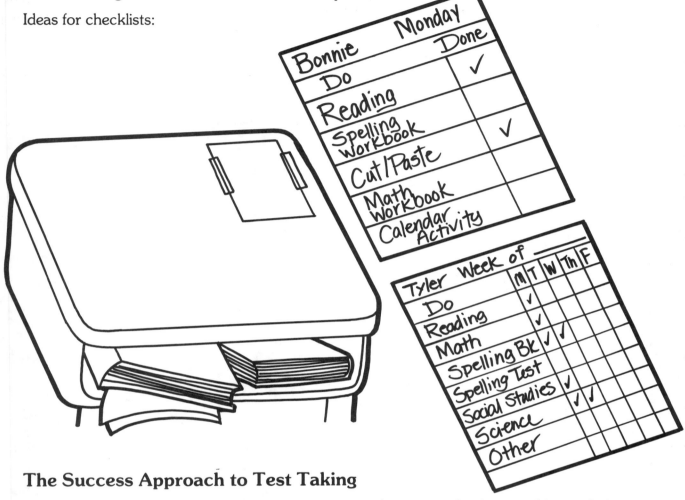

The Success Approach to Test Taking

Create an "I can do it!" attitude by teaching your students some basic test-taking techniques.

Create a sample test on a subject your students are currently studying. Include true/false, multiple choice, fill-in, and short answer questions. Duplicate the test to use with students. Teach a directed lesson on test-taking techniques.

Show students how to:

- identify and underline key words in each question;

- skip difficult questions and work on them last;

- narrow down the choices on multiple choice questions by eliminating obviously incorrect answers;

- reread each question and answer after completing the test to make sure they make sense;

- use textbooks to find answers during open-book tests.

Building Self-Esteem

Self-enhancing activities build a sense of self-worth. Students who feel good about themselves are better equipped to succeed at school. Provide opportunities for your students to build self-esteem.

FS-8310 Motivating Your Students

A Positive Touch

Good News Wristbands!

Congratulate a student with a "Good News Wristband"! Use wristbands as rewards for outstanding behavior or learning new skills. Keep strips of colorful tagboard or construction paper handy for "Good News Wristbands"!

My Best Subject

Students will enjoy a sense of accomplishment with a special book cover that rewards their achievements. Every student chooses her best subject and makes a special book cover for the text that corresponds to that subject.

Extra Special Chairs

Make a chair "extra special" by covering the back of it with a slipcover made from felt, brightly colored fabric, or a pillowcase. Use felt pens to add a title to the Extra Special Chair.

Make chair covers for:

- class officers
- birthdays
- student of the week
- special award chairs
  (See list on page 48.)

A Positive Touch

A Word of Approval

Vary the way you show approval of your students. Here's a list of words and phrases to write on worksheets or for verbal praise!

- Fantastic
- Right again
- Fabulous
- Exactly
- That's right
- Beautiful work
- All right
- Perfect
- Keep going
- Fascinating
- Delightful
- Positively correct
- Go ahead
- Brilliant
- How clever
- Remarkable
- Excellent
- Nice work
- Fine job
- I'm proud of you
- How neat
- Exciting
- Supreme
- Mighty good
- Glorious
- Grand
- Magnificent
- Superior effort
- Way to go
- That's special
- Splendid
- Superb
- Good answer
- You're on the right track
- That's the answer
- Neat work
- I love it!
- Nice handwriting
- Super-duper job

FS-8310 Motivating Your Students

All About Me

Past, Present and Future Accomplishments

Have students reflect on a special time from their past. It could be when they learned something new, received an award, or took a trip. Then have each student select a special event from the present and one she anticipates for the future. She folds a large piece of drawing paper in thirds and labels each section as shown, illustrating the three events.

You can have students write a sentence describing the illustration in each section. Younger students can dictate their sentences to you.

The Story of My Life

Students love to write about themselves. Have them make a "Story of My Life" booklet by reproducing pages 40 and 41. Encourage students to discuss important events with their families for this project. Add colorful covers to the booklets.

Allow time for students to share their booklets with others!

Story of My Life

MY name is _____

My birthday is _____ .

I was born in _____ .

I am _____ years old.

When I was a baby, I _____

_____

_____

Me As a Baby

Meet My Family

My family _____

_____

_____

_____

_____

_____

My Family

My First Day at School

On my first day of school, I _____

_____

_____

_____

_____

_____

Going to School

Having Fun

A Fun Time

For fun I like to _____
_____
_____
_____
_____
_____
_____

A Special Event

Something very special happened to me.

_____
_____
_____
_____

A Special Time

Meet My Friends

My friends _____
_____
_____
_____
_____
_____

My Friends

41

a reproducible page

All About Me

All-About-Me Bulletin Board

This fun-to-create bulletin board highlights the similarities and differences among your students. Students will enjoy reading about their classmates.

To make daisies for the bulletin board, each student cuts a circle for the center and eight petals. Stems and leaves can be cut from green paper. He draws a self-portrait or attaches a photograph on the flower's center. Then he numbers the petals from one to eight and writes information on each petal according to the posted chart.

1. My hobby

2. Favorite color

3. Future career

4. Favorite television show

5. Favorite school subject

6. Favorite game or sport

7. Favorite animal

8. Favorite food

42

All About Me

String of Hearts

Students recognize their best qualities by making a String of Hearts! Cut hearts from construction paper in pastel colors. Discuss positive qualities with your class and list them on the chalkboard. Tell students to select qualities that best describe themselves for their String of Hearts. Every child writes his qualities on separate hearts and pastes the hearts on a strip of ribbon or paper. Hearts can be decorated with "lace" cut from paper doilies.

Students can make their String of Hearts about a parent, best friend, or someone they appreciate. This activity is perfect for Mother's or Father's Day.

Look at Me Now!

Use a time capsule to record how students grow and change over the school year. In the fall, have students complete the reproducible worksheet on page 44. Collect and store the worksheets in a "time capsule" made from a shoe box. At the end of the school year, students fill out another copy of the reproducible worksheet. Then, open the time capsule and let students compare their beginning and end-of-the-year responses. Have a class discussion about how students have changed.

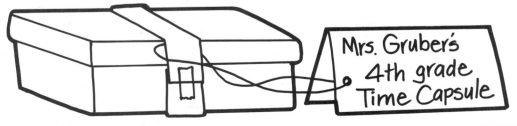

Name _____   Date _____

Look at Me Now!

Complete each sentence.

1. My favorite food is _____ .

2. My favorite song is _____ .

3. My favorite TV show is _____ .

4. When I grow up, I want to be _____ .

5. My favorite book is _____ .

6. My favorite movie is _____ .

7. My favorite school subject is _____ .

8. I wish I had a _____ .

9. I often think about _____
_____ .

10. What I'd most like to be doing is _____
_____ .

All About Me

You've Got the Cutest Baby Face!

What fun to have a baby picture derby in your classroom! Ask students to bring a baby picture to class. Display the baby pictures and number each photograph. Do not reveal the identities of the babies. Be sure to include a baby picture of yourself! Have students number their papers and try to identify their classmates from the baby pictures.

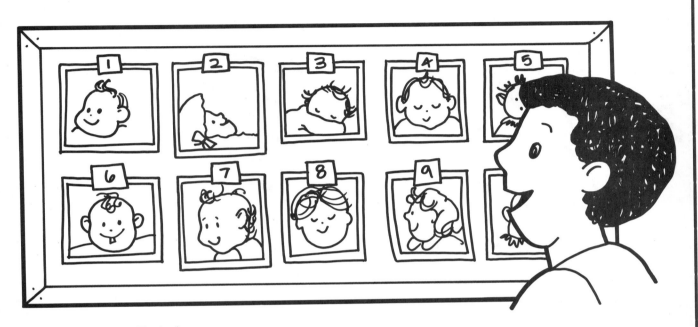

Writing on a Rainbow

Students write their opinions on a rainbow. After writing on the rainbows, have students color the rainbows according to the directions on page 46.

Rainbows can be cut out and displayed on a bulletin board or mounted on construction paper. Use the reproducible "Writing on a Rainbow" worksheet on page 46.

FS-8310 Motivating Your Students

Writing on a Rainbow

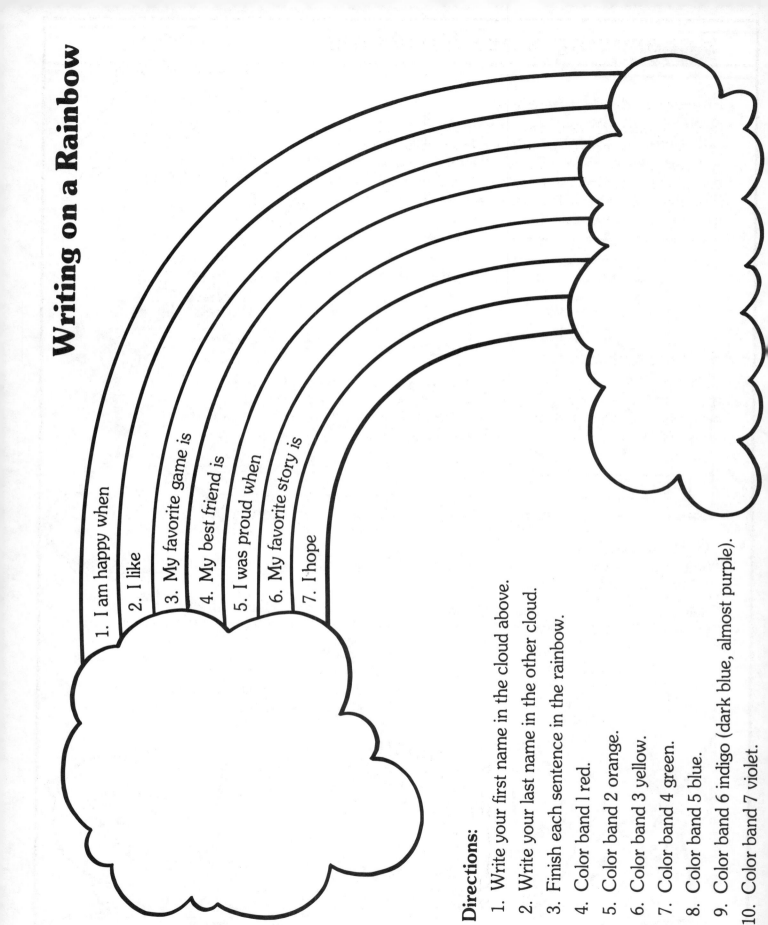

1. I am happy when
2. I like
3. My favorite game is
4. My best friend is
5. I was proud when
6. My favorite story is
7. I hope

Directions:

1. Write your first name in the cloud above.
2. Write your last name in the other cloud.
3. Finish each sentence in the rainbow.
4. Color band 1 red.
5. Color band 2 orange.
6. Color band 3 yellow.
7. Color band 4 green.
8. Color band 5 blue.
9. Color band 6 indigo (dark blue, almost purple).
10. Color band 7 violet.

FS-8310 Motivating Your Students

Reassuring Your Students

Everyone Makes Mistakes!

Reassure your students that mistakes are part of the learning process. Tell them it's common to experience some difficulty and frustration when they are learning something new. You may want to describe a situation when you experienced this frustration. Students will feel more comfortable about making mistakes when they realize it happens to everyone.

Sit Back and Enjoy It

Children need time to enjoy the mastery of a new skill. Provide opportunities for them to "take a break" before moving on to learning new skills. Let volunteers demonstrate to the class what they have learned. Have students get into small groups and share their new knowledge with each other. Allow many opportunities for students to demonstrate their new mastery to others.

You Can Do It!

Before presenting a new skill or an activity, give your class a chance to rise to the challenge.

FS-8310 Motivating Your Students

A Pat on the Back

Very Special Bookmarks

Students love to receive a personalized bookmark as a reward. Prepare an assortment of bookmarks so they are ready-to-use. Attach yarn or ribbon to construction paper cut in a variety of shapes and colors. Personalize the bookmark by adding the child's name and a positive comment.

Suggested awards:

- Kindness
- Taking Turns
- Cooperation
- Enthusiasm
- Citizenship
- Friendship
- Responsibility
- Good Friend
- Happy Smile
- Neatness
- Happiness
- Fairness
- Dependability
- Helping Others
- Athletic
- Helper
- Doing Your Share
- Hard Worker
- Good Worker
- Artistic
- Super Reader
- Super Speller
- Math Whiz
- Science Expert
- Social Studies Expert
- Beautiful Handwriting

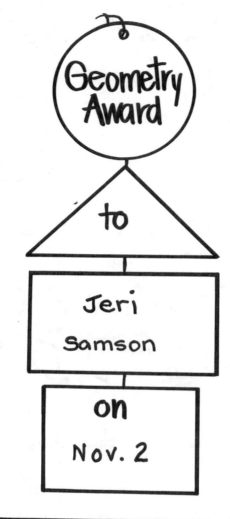

©Frank Schaffer Publications, Inc.

FS-8310 Motivating Your Students

Expressing Appreciation

A Hearty Thanks!

Create warm feelings in your classroom with a bulletin board filled with hearts.

Ask students to think about a person who helped them or did something nice for them. Give each student a heart on which you have pasted lined writing paper. Every child writes a few sentences describing an act of kindness and the person's name on a heart. Make the hearts extra fancy by adding yarn, ribbon, and lace cut from paper doilies. Display the hearts on a bulletin board as shown.

Thank-You Notes

Jot a quick note of appreciation to a student who was helpful or kind. Keep a supply of thank-you notes handy. Use the reproducible notes on page 50. These notes come in handy for thanking colleagues and parents, too!

To:

Thank you for

_____

_____

Appreciation
Award
to

_____

for _____

_____

_____

from

_____

Thank you

_____

_____

_____

_____

Thanks a bunch!

_____

_____

FS-8310 Motivating Your Students

Student Opinions Count

Read This Book!

Encourage students to share opinions about books they have read. Students can show the books to the class and tell why they liked them. They may want to recommend some of the books to others.

Your Opinion, Please!

It is important for students to know that their opinions count! Take a class poll on an issue important to your students. Use the reproducible worksheet "Your Opinion, Please!" on page 52. Jot the topic on the top of one or two sheets and pass them around the class. Every student writes her answer or opinion in a talk bubble with her name or initials.

Consider stapling several "Your Opinion, Please!" surveys into a Class Opinion Book.

Perhaps students can suggest topics for the survey.

Your Opinion, Please, About _____

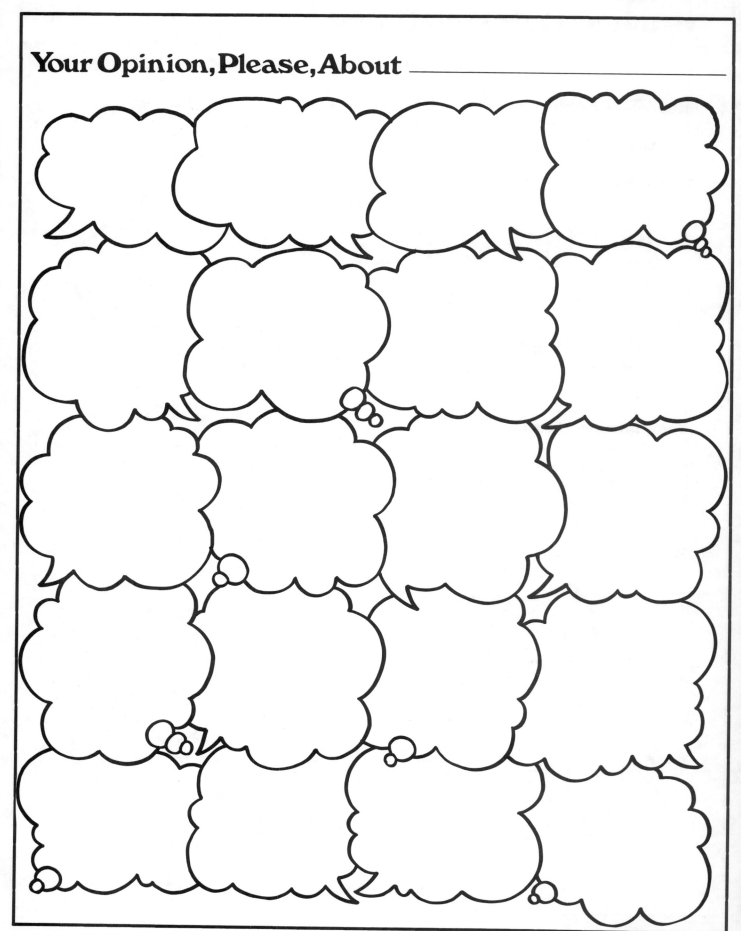

FS-8310 Motivating Your Students

a reproducible page

Emphasize the Positive

Oh, Happy Day!

Emphasize the positive events in the school day by making a Happy Happenings diary! Each student makes a booklet with a colorful cover. She decorates the booklet cover with a happy theme. Tell students to record things they have seen or heard that day that made them feel happy. Students can draw pictures or write sentences about the happy happenings of the day!

It's "Kindness Month"!

Any month can be "Kindness Month"! Lead a class discussion about kindness. Explain to the students that you will be on the lookout for kind behavior during "Kindness Month." Keep a pad of paper handy to jot down a quick note whenever you observe a child being kind. Slip the note into a special "Kindness Box." Encourage students to put notes in the box about kind deeds they observe.

At the end of each week read the notes aloud. Students can take Kindness Notes home to share.

    FS-8310 Motivating Your Students

Students in the Limelight

Fun Photos!

Did you know that you can photocopy photographs? Copy color or black and white photos of individuals or groups. Students love seeing their very own photographs all around the classroom.

Photocopied pictures can be used for:

- name tags
- award certificates
- art projects
- greeting cards
- letters to pen pals
- whole class graphing activities
- personal stationery
- class yearbooks
- bookmarks
- autograph books
- good-work bulletin boards
- covers for booklets, journals, scrapbooks ...
- helper charts
- thank-you notes
- booklets for classmates who are ill or moving away
- mailboxes/cubby holes

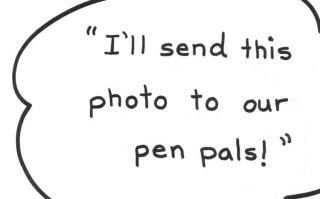

FS-8310 Motivating Your Students

Students in the Limelight

My Yearbook

Students will treasure these special yearbooks! Staple paper (construction paper, white paper, or newsprint) into a booklet for each student. Reproduce the yearbook worksheet on page 56. Have students color and cut out the headings, pasting one on each yearbook page.

Pictures

Remember When

MY TEACHER

OUR SCHOOL

Something Funny...

My Favorite Moment

Autographs

My Yearbook

NAME

GRADE

Reward Your Students

The Chance Drawing!

Looking for an opportunity to accentuate the positive in your classroom? Catch your students doing something good and reward them with a "Chance Slip." Hold a weekly drawing for prizes! The Chance Slip drawing rewards good behavior. It's exciting, fun, and costs nothing.

Duplicate and cut apart the Chance Slips on page 58. Store them in a shoe box on your desk. Students can earn Chance Slips by:

- working quietly
- obeying silent reading rules
- exhibiting good behavior in the library
- displaying good behavior in the cafeteria
- following directions on field trips
- cleaning up well after an art activity
- quietly practicing spelling words or math facts
- waiting patiently in line
- returning a signed permission slip

Hand out Chance Slips intermittently so they retain their appeal and interest remains high. Children write their name on the back of Chance Slips. Students enter the drawing by placing as many Chance Slips as they wish in a container for the end-of-the-week drawing.

Hold a weekly Chance Slip drawing on Friday afternoons. Students decide if they wish to participate and how many of their Chance Slips to enter. Add to the excitement by keeping the assortment of prizes a secret until Chance Slips are deposited in the container. The student whose name is drawn first gets to select one prize from the assortment. The second student whose name is drawn gets to select one prize from the remaining prizes.

Prizes are free goodies you have collected such as:

- free stationery or note pads
- breakfast cereal premiums
- items from teachers' conventions (bookmarks, pencils,...)
- premiums from banks and stores (balloons, bumper stickers, ...)
- chance slip holders (candy tins and boxes)
- coupons for class privileges
- book-club premiums
- murals, books, and banners (made by your students)

Chance	**Chance**	**Chance**
Chance	**Chance**	**Chance**
Chance	**Chance**	**Chance**
Chance	**Chance**	**Chance**
Chance	**Chance**	**Chance**
Chance	**Chance**	**Chance**
Chance	**Chance**	**Chance**
Chance	**Chance**	**Chance**

FS-8310 Motivating Your Students

a reproducible page

Reach Out Beyond Your Classroom

Adopt a Class!

Adopt a class at your school for a few weeks or for the whole school year. Your adoptive class can be younger, older, or a special education or gifted class. Plan special activities to enjoy together.

- Host a let's-get-acquainted event.
- Play a P.E. game together.
- Eat lunch together.
- Have a library period together.
- Take a hike around the school together.
- Visit each other's class for a lesson.
- Take a field trip together.
- See a film together.
- Exchange greeting cards.
- Prepare food and have a picnic.
- Take photographs of your adoptive class.
- Make a seasonal or holiday banner for the class.
- Read books together.
- Do cross-age tutoring.
- Teach an indoor-recess game.
- Have a sing-along.
- Have a wrap-up party at the end of the year.

FS-8310 Motivating Your Students

Reach Out Beyond Your Classroom

Instant Public Relations!

Increase students' pride in their work and team spirit by giving them special attention. After students have completed a special project, seek out some free publicity from:

- local or city newspapers
- local radio stations
- local television stations
- the school newsletter
- PTA bulletins

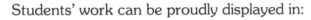

Students' work can be proudly displayed in:

- the local post office
- community businesses
- shopping malls
- city hall
- the school principal's office
- the school district office
- school or public libraries
- the cafeteria
- the computer lab
- PTA meetings
- school

Fostering Self-Esteem

Snap a Picture!

Snap a roll of pictures in your classroom at different times during the school day. Make sure each child appears in at least one picture. It might be fun to include the school principal in one or two photographs. Post the photos on a bulletin board entitled "Our Class in Action!" Print captions on construction paper and post them under the photos.

Instead of using a bulletin board, photos and captions can be pasted in a construction paper booklet.

People I Admire

Tell your students about a man and woman you admire. Describe the qualities that make these people admirable. Then, give students the "People I Admire" reproducible worksheet on page 62. Have every child write the names of two people he admires and list each person's qualities.

The shapes on page 62 can be colored to resemble the actual people. Allow time for students to share their work.

Name _____ Date _____

People I Admire

I admire

_____
because he is
_____
_____
_____
_____
_____
_____
_____
_____
_____

I admire

_____
because she is
_____
_____
_____
_____
_____
_____
_____
_____
_____
_____

62

FS-8310 Motivating Your Students

a reproducible page